Tonight the Moon is Red

Virginia McKenna

Tonight The Moon Is Red

Book and cover design by Alex Whitworth
Illustrations by Alex Whitworth

The following poems were published in 1999 in the
Born Free Foundation's Anniversary Collection:
What is the Earth?
Solitude
Otter
Memories
Darkness Comes Again
Rainbow Elephants
Leopard
Wolf
The Field
Dolphin reprinted by kind permission of Harper Collins

www.muswell-press.co.uk

To my beloved family, to my Born Free family, to my friends and to all the animals who deserve our kindness and respect.

Contents:

Memories and Reflections

Tonight The Moon Is Red

There is the honesty of passion in the poetry of Virginia McKenna, openly declared, open-hearted. There is the fire of love, of loyalty and of anger too. This does not make easy reading. Every poem challenges, many hurt us - as they should. We flinch with her at the cruelty and exploitation of innocence, of beauty. We weep with her at the loss and the suffering and the longing.

Yet we can feel, as she does, through it all, the hope and the beauty and the essential goodness in man and we can rejoice with her in this conviction. But we know that it takes people like her, whose life and work is an inspiration to so many, to bring out that goodness; to enable us to make this the best of all possible worlds, for us, our fellow creatures and for the planet itself. She has fought the good fight, and these poems are her battle cries.

Michael Morpurgo OBE, April 2014

Wilderness and Wildlife

Kenya holds some of the memories I most treasure.
The ever-changing skies, the smell of earth after rain, the myriad creatures, surviving as they can. And, of course, I always remember the people; their kindness and warmth, and seeing the challenges they face.

But my love of wild and wildlife has no boundaries – Scottish seashores, English forests – no matter where, we must cherish it.

What is the Earth

What is the earth?
A ball in space?
A little paradise?
Planet of melting ice
And inner fires?

Under my hand
Its surface crumbles
Crushed underfoot
Its myriad flowers.

Forests lie trembling
Under my sword
The ocean darkens
Weeping black tears.

Death of sweet rivers
Death-giving rain
Silent and secret
Invisible pain.

A gift from heaven
This little world
Each bird a jewel
Each tree a mother.

What is the earth?
A fragile heart.
Tender my touch
To save its life –
And mine.

Friends

When I return to Africa
It is with friends.
Friends from other journeys,
Other times.
Our hearts beat as one
Seeing mountains
With the same eyes
Smelling sun-baked earth
With the same joy
Our minds opening
In the same way
To new people
Strange encounters
Deep feelings.
Africa binds us.
Inexplicably.

What lies beyond the hill?
Do thorn trees shade
Those mammoth giants?
Will starlings so superb greet
Our wide gaze
As myriad images of nature
Crowd the scene?
This land so old and yet
So full of birth
This land where life began.
How poignant is its skein
Around our hearts.

Dew – damp cobwebs
Thread the dawn grass
Cry of fish eagle
Roar of lion
Call of hyena
Pierce the air
Haunting our souls forever.
Friendship around the fire
Burns deep.
Beneath the night's dark ceiling
Daisied with stars
We talk and smile.
And share the silence.
Remembering the day.

Darkness Comes Again

In my mind's eye, bird's eye,
I see the African plains.
Dry, huge, far as the eye of whatever kind
Can see.

Mountains on the edge of the sky
Stand violet and inviolate
Sentinels stretching to clouds.
Clouds forever changing the space pattern of blue.

Thornbush, acacia,
Umbrella pools of sanctuary and shade
In noon-day fire.
Grey coolness harbouring grey majesty
Of elephants.
Nature's monarchs.
Nature's great teachers.

Trunks curling and caressing.
Ears giant palm leaves,
Fanning,
To cool the noon-hot blood.
Wise eyes, lash-curtained,
High foreheads, noble.
Harbouring an ancient store of memories.

Flash of ivory amongst the grey.
Ivory-coloured prizes.
Coveted for carvings.
Unthroning mammoth kings and queens alike.
Returning all to dust.

My mind's eye weeps for you
As you fall to the earth.
My small heart bleeds for yours
As your blood is spilled.

Red blood, splattering the earth
And thirst-racked thorns.
Scarlet on ivory
Momentarily.
Then snatched away to light some vaulted store.
The ivory gleam has gone.
And darkness comes again to Africa.

Rainbow Elephants

The elephants are blue
Blue in the evening's indigo
The dawn's first azure light.

The elephants are red
Red from the terracotta soil's
Warm wallowed mantle.

The elephants are silver
Moon ghosts between the trees
And shining through night's veil.

The elephants are grey
Without disguise of light or night
Grey shadows in the forest.

The elephants are gone
Mourned spirits in the air
Haunting our dreams.

Ring of Bright Water

So many times I'd thought,
Imagined, dreamed
Of where the ring
First shimmered in the sun.
And now a greater ring
Encompassed me
As Camusfearna entered in my soul.

A million shells cushioned my eager step
And beckoned me to kneel
And seek the ones
To place upon the graves
With other treasures, gathered from the shore.

It seemed to me
The spirit of those long-gone days
Had touched each fragment
Of that magic place
The dunes, the whispering grass,
The turning tide, the grey-white
Clouds, which architect the sky.

Although I saw no otters swim and play
Their joyous image filled the quiet air
With cries and squeaks which echoed through the
Hours.

This day, these moments
Now are part of me
Until that time when I will be no more
But spin in space somewhere beyond the stars.

Otter

I lift this moment in my outstretched palm
And carry it beyond the shores of time.

And so in deepest dark, tumultuous crowds,
On solitary trail
Or in the secret womb of lonely hours
I see the otter with its sleek, brown head
Breaking the surface of the racing tide
And plunging east towards the rising sun.

The first pale shafts spear peaks of distant hills,
Tempting our hearts to leap and meet the day.

And slowly, as the cloth of gold descends
On pristine fields of brilliant crystal snow,
Fades from our view the fickle goddess moon
Gifting her light on other, distant shores.

Wolf

I thrill to your
Primaeval call
I imagine your head
Tipped back
Vulnerable neck
Eyes closed
Straining to reach
The sky
Connect
To a distant mate.

The darkness
Echoes
Stars plummet
Wildly, silently.
My heart pounds.

Dawn finds you
Encircling
Your land,
Marking, hunting,
Protecting your family.
Far from myth
False fable
Red-cloaked girl.

Beautiful
Your untamed
Wildness.
Keep calling
To the moon
Keep free.
From us.

The Fear That Has No Name

Fear of the hare as it runs for its life
Fear of the lamb as it faces the knife
Fear of the bird as it's trapped in its cage
Fear of the dog of its master's rage

Fear of the fox as it hears 'tally ho'
Fear of the whale as the harpoon strikes low
Fear of the wolf as it flees from the gun
Fear of the bear as it 'dances' for fun

Fear of the badger dug out of its lair
Fear of the animal caught in a snare
Fear of the elephant as poachers give chase
Fear of all creatures when dangers they face.

Fear for ourselves. When the reckoning comes.

Nature's Magic

Everything falls into place
When I see the leaves turning,
Flame, russet, glorious gold.
The autumn blazens its trail
Above the path I tread.
That path is cushioned
With fallen signs of summer
Papery whisps of hay, and conkers,
And twigs of oak, snapped
By the untamed wind.

I know the world is circling
On the seasons' great clock
Whose hands are sure,
Untouchable, reassuring.
On this day, when writing this,
I need that confirmation.
I need to know that nature
Is steadfast. Dependable. Honest.
Believing, as I do, in man's goodness
Being, as I am, an optimist,
I am, against my will, feeling
A fading in my inner life force.
A force, till now, so strong, so full of hope.
Some weeks from now the branches
Will lie bare, the ferns died back
The streams dancing with winter rain.
I shall walk that path again
And let the comfort of the forest
Enter my heart. And, who can tell,
Return me back to life.

Tonight the Moon is Red

Tonight The Moon Is Red

Some of these poems are recent but old, or new, they are, in a way, joined up thinking. Bombarded on television and radio by tragic stories of suffering and combat and loss and fear it is impossible not to be affected by the relentless messages.
But, for me, life has to be about balance. So our eyes must open ever wider to the beauty of nature and the exquisite images she gifts us.

Talking

There is a man in a room
Talking.
I hear him. Talking.
The people sit. Silent.
Listening.
What it is about?
The stars? The sea?
The meaning of life?
Death?
He has a grey suit.
Neat.
He has a grey voice.
Monotone
What is he saying?
It has no theme.
Why is he saying it?
I could be outside
Under the trees
By the river
Lying in a field
Listening to nature.
A speech must have
A theme
A central argument.
Otherwise it is just a man
In a room.
Talking.

Interview

They were on TV
The mother. The father.
Their daughter was dead.
'How do you feel?'
Said the presenter.
How do you feel
When your daughter
Is dead? Murdered.
How could that question
Be asked?
And how, on TV
Can they expose
Their breaking hearts?
The years they face
Without the child
Born out of love –
Scream out their pain?
'Could you forgive him?'
Said the presenter –
(Perfect make-up and hair
Light years from comprehension).
'We could start to try'
Said the mother.
A Saint of our time.

Day of Remembering

Both glad and sad
Times
Day of recalling
Both sweet and bitter
Sweet.

Do son-less men
Yearn to be fathers
As
Arms of childless
Women burn with
Emptiness?

Fathers long gone
Fathers with families
And
Fathers, alone,
Or waiting in the wings
Unknowing.

Mark the day
With flowers, with love
And
Treasure the man
Who brought you into
Life.

Father's Day - June

Farewell to Flowers

My heart will burst
He thought
Her hand so frail
Touching the flowers

The petals falling
Drifting down
The fingers trembling.
Sweetly. Painfully.

What strength it took
This last farewell
Leaving behind
Treasures so loved.

Engraved forever
Upon his soul
The beauty of flowers
Touched by her love.

Unfair Game

You mean – hunting lions?
Elephants? Deer? Foxes?
Shooting migrating birds
From hill-top hides?
Yes, that's right –
How did you guess?

Well, that's what man does.
Isn't it? Kills for fun.
Macho man in macho gear.
Oh, good shot! Clean Shot!
It will look great on the wall,
On the floor, draped on the chair.
Eyes seeing no more. Heart arrested.
But the man, of course, is free.

Will it haunt him in the night?
Don't be crazy. As I write
He is dreaming of the next
Life he can steal. Broad daylight too.

Oh man, how small you are
How tiny in the scheme of things.
You are not rare and beautiful
Like the lion, the elephant, the deer,
The soaring birds. It is not you
Who fills our hearts with wonder and with joy.
And when you've killed them all –
What then?

Our Land

Hard to say nowadays
What it is to be
British.
Is it the horrors of hooliganism
Football and internet 'grooming'
Is it Neighbourhood Watch and compassion?
Possibly.
The pastel colours of our race
Now mix with vibrant tones
From other lands
Wonderful.
To be British is anything and everything.
Probably.
For me though it is the land itself
That stirs my heart.
My loyalty.
Our forests, fields, wild coasts
And yes, roses around the door
And washing in the wind.
To be truly British you love your land.
Completely.

Everything

You see, it's not about that. Out there. Warnings. Oh
God
Warnings. Terror.
Fear. On the streets.
Watch that bag. Is it yours?
Suspicious. Cross the road.
He looks odd. More than designer stubble.
I can smell… I can sense him.

It's about this. Trees turning gold.
Ice dawns. Frost like snow.
Birds sheltering. Feeding.
Horses in the field
With blanketed backs.
Breath a vapour trail.

In fact, it's about everything
Dark and light. Sun and shadow.
Joy and pain. Sweet and bitter.
Nothing remains forever.
And we do have choice.
Don't we?
We can open the robin's cage.
Silence the guns. Let the dolphins swim free.
Bring comfort not sorrow. Turn the other cheek.
Can't we?
Although I am old
I am leaping inside. Huge steps.
Imploring, begging, hoping
That people will see the snow,
Embrace the dawn.
Put fear in its place.
Let the robin go.

Tonight The Moon Is Red

Tonight the Moon is Red
Flaming the night sky
What do I see?
A sign? An omen?
A Fateful Message
Of the blood
So soon to spill
Upon the earth?
Our earth
Our little planet
So loved, so vulnerable,
So tortured.
What is to come?
Mothers, as I am
Shrieking their pain
As babies, children,
Glorious young men
Spill their red moon blood
Upon the thirsty soil.

Tonight the Moon is Red

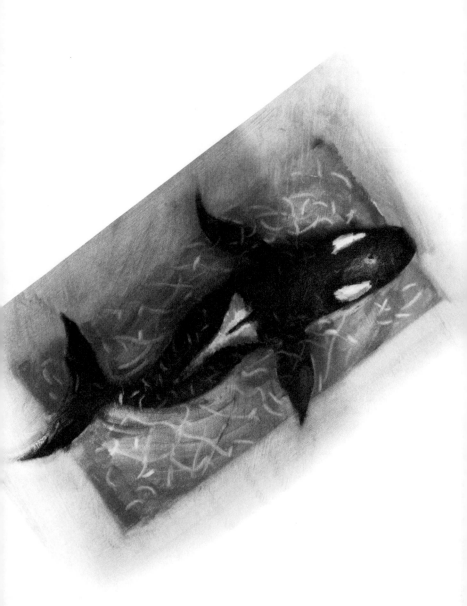

Captives

In the work I have been involved in over the past thirty years
with our charity, The Born Free Foundation, my personal focus
has always been on wild animals in captivity. Having been
fortunate to visit Africa many times, and to see them in their true
environment, watching them existing in zoos and circuses was
extremely difficult. It still is. Of course, some captive facilities
are better than others, it would be unreasonable to say otherwise.
But, whatever the situations, and however tough and challenging
'the wild' is, that is where wild creatures belong.

My poems in this section were all written after personal visits
to different places. Animals Asia rescue centres in China and
Vietnam (and bear 'farms' in Vietnam); a zoo in Hong Kong, now
closed, the zoo in Addis Ababa, Ethiopia; two zoos in England;
a visit to Seaworld in Florida many years ago. (Thankfully a
documentary film *Blackfish* has recently revealed the truth
behind the music and tricks of dolphinaria). We do not have
the 'right' to see everything and no animal should suffer for one
momentary glance.

The Darkest Day

I made this journey aware
Of what I would find. Would see.
I thought I was prepared.
But nothing can. No film. No words.
Nor these few lines of mine
Can wrench your heart and haunt your mind
As seeing it yourself.

No words can really tell you.
Should I say torment?
Cruelty? Despair? Hell on earth?
Shall I say prison? Torture?
Nightmare? Madhouse?
Nothing screams out the obscenity
Of those barbaric traps.
Yes. Traps of bars - above,
Beside, beneath, no floor
On which to rest those
Rotting, yellowed feet..
The feet of bears who carry still
The precious moons emblazoned
On their night-dark chests.

This moon is all they have.
There is no sun to lighten
That grim shed, no trees
To soothe the eye, no wind
To stir their fur, no hope
Of kinder days. And why?
It is the bile. Of course, it is the bile.
Extracted, traded, packaged
And sold in pretty phials
For "mankind's" benefit. No kindness here.
Some bears are mad. I know
The signs too well. They sway and rock
And twist. Seeking oblivion.
Even for a minute. Even for a moment.

And then, oh God, this bear I saw.
A huge great glorious beast
Stretched out across the bars.
His back legs up against the side,
His two front legs reached high,
As if to heaven, stretched high and still
Until, suddenly, a paw dropped down
And grabbed his slavering tongue,
And pulled and pulled it out
And out again until I thought
It surely would snap free.
But no, the paw jerked up
Once more - and on and on again.

These dark satanic sheds
Are known as farms. Death Row
I say. Outside the owners offer tea.
I want to put them in a cage
And let them cry. In vain.

Not all these innocent creatures
Will find sanctuary. There are thousands.
Only a few will walk on grass,
Climb trees, feel sun and wind. Be loved.

And, as I stood, aghast, the eye
Of one sweet bear looked into mine.
Unflinching. Enduring. Stoic.
Yes, that is the word I seek.
I heard it many times. The stoicism
Of these great animals. And, miraculously,
The rescued ones appear to feel
No malice, bear no grudge, as if
They sense the kindness shown
The affection given.

In all the years I have watched
Imprisoned animals - some neglected,
Some abused, some stir-crazy,
All helpless - this November day
Has been the darkest of them all.
And what a lesson have I learned.
How dare I now complain of cold,
Or tiredness, or waiting for a train?
On behalf of all who cause
This purgatory, I hang my head in shame
And beg the bears' forgiveness in my heart.

Tonight the Moon is Red

The Sanctuary

The moon I love the most
Is not the gleaming ball
Of iridescent light
Sailing the night sky.

The moon I love the most
Rides on the night-dark chests
Of wild black bears,
Sometimes pure white,
Or ivory or cream.
Its crescent marks these beasts
Sublimely. Tragically.

These are the chosen ones
Victims of man's callous need
For cures. Bile in a bottle.
Elixir to end his pain.

But for the trapped moon bears
The pain is endless
Taps turn. Tubes drip.
The cage an iron glove.
Torment is infinite.

Yet here around me,
At the Sanctuary,
There is the sweetest sight.
Bears play and sleep
And shuffle as they will
They feel the air and smell the rain.
And learn that human-kind
Can be just that.

How humble we should be
To have their trust
How steadfast we must be
To change men's hearts
So all the crescent moons,
Imprisoned still,
Can shine once more.

The Bleeding Heart Baboon in the Zoo

They call me Gelada baboon.
They say my bleeding heart
Is on my breast.
Neither is true.
I am a primate of a different sort.
My flaming breast reveals
My sexual state.
But no one sees my heart
It is within. Burning in its pain
Bursting in its grief.

They laugh and point
And mock my shrunken life.
My poverty of life
In this bare cell.
Killing my instincts
Suffocating my senses
My breast no more alight
But pale and dim as twilight.

In nature I am a mzee
A wise elder of the troop
Caring for the young.
But here, for no one.
And no one cares for me.
I hope my heart will break.

Addis Ababa

Solitude

I am in my room, alone,
Time is nothing.
The silence and its stillness pleases me.

I can keep this solitude
Without question,
Until the need to end it pleases me.

In his small cage, alone,
Time is nothing.
His silence is within, inside his brain,
He keeps this inward silence
To protect him
From eyes that do not understand his pain.

I keep him in this cage
My primate brother,
I keep him on display for all to see.
I must be sure that he knows
Who is master,
That in my hand, alone, lies freedom's key.

Reflections

Inside the palm, under the searching fingers
The skin is pink and wrinkled.
Just like mine.

Eyes behind the mesh behind the glass
Look into my eyes.
Same thoughts. I know.

Sad, mad monkey
In that twilight box.
Reflected in the glass,
Dim outline in that silent, sordid world
I see myself, and you beyond.
Trapped. Forever.
In my memory.

What is your question?
Why?
Mine is the same.

Leopard

That look of scorn and anger burned my soul.
The yellow orbs shone cold gold metal.
My throat closed up. I turned my head away.

Black panthers in the forest move with silken stealth
Between the trees
Feet silent as they touch the fallen leaves.
Bodies are tuned like springs
For hunting, seeking a mate, guarding their territory.
Life is dangerous but meant to be that way.

Here at Lai Chi Kok there is no forest, no fallen leaves,
No night of stars, no rain, no warming sun.
The cage of concrete, ceilinged with the same,
Allows no patterns of the light to change
The monotone of grey in that cold cell.

The shining coat of wilder days has gone
Now dry, worn thin and lifeless like the body it encases.
The crowd screams round and shouts and roars its joy.
I also scream inside my head and shout.
This wasted tragic death in life
Is one more horror to haunt me in the night.
And fifty feet away the funfair and the music
Blast raucously to split your ears.
And no one gives a damn.

Dolphin

Mona Lisa of oceans.
Your sunshine smile beguiles
Enchants and gathers us
Into your silver-sprayed
Arc-en-ciel.

In ocean or pool your joy
Blinds us to your secrets.
Your glistening beauty,
Your tolerance of us –
Who also hide behind a mask of mirth –
Pierce the hearts of some who watch
The chlorine-scented show,
Far from the dolphin's deep and distant home
Light years from its origins
In nature's amphitheatre.

They say the elephant weeps salt tears.
The dolphin, creature of salt expanses,
Conceals its pain.
Locked in its smile as hopelessly
As we have land-locked it,
In concrete worlds of artificial sea.

Tonight the Moon is Red

Memories and reflections

Some of these poems are, perhaps, among the most personal I have written. When someone you love dies you can often be asked endless questions about your loss and how you feel. I am not opposed to revealing my feelings but I prefer to do it in my own way and in my own words.

That is why some of my poems remembering my husband Bill are here, together with some thoughts of journeys we shared.

Joy Remembered

One thing we know
One thing is sure
That we must die
And be no more.

Into the dark
Of grave and ground
Where there's no light
Where there's no sound.

What will you say
When I am gone
What will you tell
Our little son?

Speak not of worms
Of cold and clay
Of sightless eyes
And heart's decay.

Let him remember
Warmth and joy
While he is still
A little boy.

Born Again

'Are you an actress?' she said.
'Oh … yes'
Part time
Sometime
Hardly ever.
Once, upon a time.

In brave and fearless roles
Fighting the wartime foe
Living with lions
Facing with ever-so British sangfroid
The trials of life.
But now?

All talk of
What shall I wear
Look like
Speak like
Be like
Fade into meaningless mumbo.
Faceless I prefer to remain
But powerful in spirit
And voice.
Speaking for those that speak not
Fighting for those who are chained
Forced into servitude
Innocent
Helpless.

What is the purpose of life?
We all ask the same.
To do what you can
To be what you are
To care and to love.
With all your immeasurable faults
This is all you can do.

Zanskar

Twenty four years since
I picked these flowers,
They are perfect still,
Framed, dried, on the wall

Twenty four years since
We reached the Pass
Mountains to right and left.
Air crystalline, pure, sunshine bright
And the flowers, nestling
In rocks, hiding shyly
Between the rocks and the stones.
True survivors of life's harsh
And vibrant challenges.

Just here and there I picked
A tiny plant and pressed it,
Uncomplaining between the papers.
Special treasures from that climb,
That breath-taking, eye-widening
Trek, up and beyond the shrine flags.
At sixteen thousand feet,
Are we nearer to heaven?
Who knows. My little gifts
Live still upon my wall
Unfaded sweet reminders
Of the moments when
I almost touched the stars.

These flowers were picked by Bill and Virginia
in Zanskar, Northern India, in 1987

Just a Memory

I must remember
This
She thinks picking
The flower

His eyes watching
Me
My hands snapping
The stem

His lips parting
To speak
Mine brushing in silence
The petals.

Memories

Did I imagine
The heron
At first flight
Standing silver and tall
Where jetty touches sea
And then
Aroused by breeze,
Skim silently
Towards the distant shore?

Did I dream of the oyster catchers
Jetting by the boat
Their calls and cries
Echoing in the sky,
Tugging the heart
As sweetest music
Opens up our soul
To yearning and to tears?

For now I am so far
From where I wish to be
My body and my mind
In different worlds
My head awash with different images
Of sky and clouds
Of pale pale budding trees
And wind, swirling scarves and hair to heaven.

Wild strawberries beside the woodland path
High, wide archways in the soaring cliffs
Waves pounding
On the grey and pebbled beach
Memories of childhood crystal sharp and clear.
Those memories are true
Not stuff of dreams.
And so I know
The footprint on the sand
The clutch of shells upon the silent grave
The iris carpet soon to burst its gold
The crashing waterfall
The unseen hands that crush my breath
And fill my eyes with water from the deep
Are real and living and part of me.

Highland Magic

I will always remember
This September.

Rowan trees aflame
On the hills
Branches groaning
With berries.

Winter store for birds
And jars of jelly
For the picking.

Slipping down gullies,
Through bracken,
Stumbling over stones
Canopied by emerald cushions.

Gulls on the wing
Herons on the shoreline
Cries echoing in the blue
Mocking my clumsy path.

The dogs watched
As I filled my bags
Impatient to hurtle
Down the heathered track.

Harvest over
We sat perched high
On a stony hill
Together, content, silent.

The Lightness of Being

Only yesterday
We hovered like fireflies
Over aquamarine cathedrals of light
And iridescent silver.

Only yesterday
We silently streaked
Through submarine grottoes of deepest shade
And lightest light.

Shy visitors
Loosened from our feet of clay
Skimming like thistledown
On Neptune's liquid ceiling.

Seductive fingers
Of sea plants waved and beckoned
From secret moorings in the flickering sand
Elusive sirens forever songless.

And now today
I close my eyes against the sun
I dream my dreams beneath the stars
And gaze forever at that magic world.

For John and Colette

C'est comme tu dormais
Le front sans rides
Les mains calmes.
Je touche la joue.

Je t'embrasse
Mes lèvres chaudes
Sur ta peau fraiche
Où es-tu?
Ton corps n'est plus
L'abri de ton âme –
Elle vole au ciel
Elle court parmi les étoiles
Elle nous entoure,
Avec une bague de tendresse.
Elle est partout.
Ne t'eloignes pas trop.
Tiens la main de Colette
Qui a tenu la tienne,
Avec une telle dévotion
C'est dur effacer
Dans un instant
Les liens d'une vie.

Quant à nous
Ta famille
Tu ne changeras jamais
Cet oncle si beau
Charmant, amiable.
Un gentilhomme suranné.
Merci pour ton amitié
Et merci à Dieus
Pour ta vie.

Anniversary

I have no gifts nor precious toy
To mark this special day.
No flowers, no fruits, no sweetmeats rare
No songs for you to play.

The only thing I have to give
Is of a doubtful hue –
Some black, some grey, a little white
Some red, some dark deep blue.

Upon my outstretched hand it lies
This present from your wife
Please take it and its pain, its joy
It's – with my love – my life.

Yours

Whose is this hand you hold in yours?
It's yours.

Whose is the smile reflecting yours?
It's yours.

Whose are the eyes that meet your own?
The dreams you dream, the joys you've known,
The sadness you have never shown?
All yours.

In darkest hour, and brightest sun,
In morning light, when day is done,
Since first we met, we two are one.

For everything that's mine
Is yours.

Metamorphosis

I think it is quite easy to disappear
If you are still and hardly breathe
Hardly anyone will notice you.

In other times I thought I would mind
Being invisible
Now I'm not so sure.

And of course nothing stays the same
The seasons don't so why should we.

The soft green lace of spring soon turns
To dazzling summer and autumn's glowing reds
Quite soon reveal the vulnerable shapes
Of winter boughs.

When you are young the sword of your ideals
Is always bright
Always at the ready.
You really did believe the world needed you
And it made you feel that your touch
Could heal all.

Now I think I can serve it best
By taking up as little space
As a body needs.

In any case
They're cutting all the trees
Soon we won't know what the season is.

Facing the Facts

The trouble with me
Is at sixty-six
I'm still a child
That likes to run and pick up sticks
And race with the dog
In the dawn.

The trouble with me
Is at sixty-six
I'm still a girl
Who wants to touch and feel and hold
Who senses the quickening pulse
Of the spring.

The trouble with me
Is at sixty-six
I find it hard
To say adieu to the need of strong arms
And the sharing of time
As it flies.

What else can we do
But smile as we yearn
And accept we are old
And remember the touch and the feel and the kiss
That awakened our hearts
And turned midnight to gold.

Alone

Her head was down
Hidden behind the book.
Reading? Sleeping?
Weeping?
He, beside her,
Unaware.
Until her body's messages
Connected
And he turned
Saw
And, tenderly,
Kissed her cheek.
Held her close.

Now how alone I feel
No body next to mine
To feel my tears.
No arms to hold me close
Against the dark.
That's what I miss
The arms. And the kiss.

Mourning

I'm playing at life
It's a game
No winners
Just more of the same.

Filling the space
The space
Pacing the cage
Turning the page.

To the next day
Night
And following dawn
Taking a breath
And letting it out.
Right?

Empty is empty
Full is full
Nothing is nothing
And time does not heal.

I still feel your hand
Hear your voice
On the wind
In the air.

My world's a balloon.
One prick will suffice.

Lark Ascending
For Iona Brown

The notes that soared,
That music on the wing
Transported all my grief beyond the stars.

And from your magic hands
A gossamer thread of sound
Entwined its healing skeins around my heart.

Your spirit too appeared to fly
Above the heavy walls of church and town
Into the lark's domain.

How beautiful, how poignant and how rare
Those fleeting moments when our souls can sing
And tenderness and love inspire the day.

Old Age

So strange to see,
This old hand.
And it is mine!
I stir and wash
And plant and prune
And this old hand is there – before me.
Veined and wrinkled
Marked with signs of age
Nails unpolished.
No pretentions.
But once – years ago
You held this hand.
And on it placed
Two rings. I wear them
With an aching love.
I treasure them beyond
All hopes and dreams.

Small Thoughts in Spring

I am nearly eighty.
Sitting one evening
Looking at the blossom
New life
Spring life
And the fading sun
So gentle. So sweet.
I wonder if my day's
Ending will be like that.
Who knows.
And, after all,
Eighty is wonderful
Old but wonderful.
I am so lucky
Still to see the blossom
The fading sun
The new life
I am blessed
I know that.

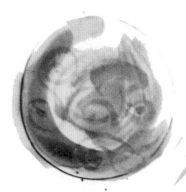

Bubbles

Some are bubble blowers
Some are bubble breakers

Have you blown bubbles
In the countryside?

The world's a bubble too

One day someone will come along
And prick the world.

The Field

What colour is the field?
Corn gold, snow white, grass green, earth brown?
No matter.
It is the womb, the grave.
The larder of both wild and human beasts.
It is your quiet space
From which your thoughts can seek their path
To heaven.

Sit silent in the field.
Open your mind and heart.
Wait for the sign.
The butterfly that lights upon your hand.
The leaf that falls from one far-distant tree.
The poignant music from the blackbird's throat.
Be still.
He will be there.

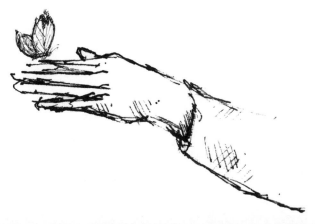